Fiddle Time Sprinters

T0086901

A third book of pieces for violin

Kathy and David Blackwell

Welcome to **Fiddle Time Sprinters.** You'll find:

- pieces using the finger pattern 01–2–34, plus low 2nd fingers and high 3rd fingers
- 2nd and 3rd position pieces
- a range of bowing techniques, including spiccato, hooked bowing, and string crossing
- original pieces in different styles, plus well-known pieces
- pieces using modes, the chromatic and blues scales, and dominant 7ths, linking with *Fiddle Time Scales 2*
- duets with parts of equal difficulty
- CD of performances and backings, with drumkit and bass added for the jazz and rock numbers
- piano and violin accompaniments available separately.

Pieces with piano accompaniment are presented in two formats on the CD: firstly, a complete performance, then the accompaniment only, which you can play along to. There is a count-in when the violin and piano parts start together.

This symbol is placed alongside all the pieces that appear on the accompanying CD. When there are two numbers given in the symbol, the top number indicates the complete performance, and the bottom number the accompaniment alone.

In all duet pieces, the top part is assigned to the right-hand channel and the lower part to the left-hand channel. You can choose to play along with either part by muting the appropriate channel.

MUSIC DEPARTMENT

OXFORD
UNIVERSITY PRESS

OXFORD
UNIVERSITY PRESS

Great Clarendon Street, Oxford OX2 6DP,
United Kingdom

Oxford University Press is a department of the University of Oxford.
It furthers the University's aim of excellence in research, scholarship,
and education by publishing worldwide. Oxford is a registered trade mark of
Oxford University Press in the UK and in certain other countries

This collection © Oxford University Press 2003 and 2013

Kathy and David Blackwell have asserted their right under the Copyright, Designs
and Patents Act, 1988, to be identified as the Composers of this Work

Database right Oxford University Press (maker)

First published 2003

Impression: 13

All rights reserved. No part of this publication may be reproduced,
stored in a retrieval system, or transmitted, in any form or by any means,
without the prior permission in writing of Oxford University Press

Permission to perform the works in this anthology in public
(except in the course of divine worship) should normally be obtained from
a local performing right licensing organization, unless the owner or the occupier
of the premises being used already holds a licence from such an organization.
Likewise, permission to make and exploit a recording of these works
should be obtained from a local mechanical copyright licensing organization

Enquiries concerning reproduction outside the scope of the above
should be directed to the Music Rights Department, Oxford University Press, at
music.permissions.uk@oup.com or at the address above

ISBN 978–0–19–338679–2

Music and text origination by
Julia Bovee
Printed in Great Britain on acid-free paper by
Halstan & Co. Ltd, Amersham, Bucks.

Unless marked otherwise, all pieces are by Kathy and David Blackwell
and are © Oxford University Press. All traditional pieces,
and nos. 3, 11, 19, 20, 25, and 35, are arranged by Kathy and
David Blackwell and are © Oxford University Press. Unauthorized
arrangement or photocopying of this copyright material is ILLEGAL.

Contents

1. Ready to rock 4
2. Clear skies 4
3. Ode to joy (Beethoven) (*duet*) 5
4. Song from the show 6
5. Starry night 6
6. Paris café 7
7. Gaudete! (*duet*) 8
8. Jacob's dance 9
9. Sprint finish 9
10. Bolero (*duet*) 10
11. William Tell (Rossini) 11
12. Country gardens (*duet*) 12
13. You and me (*duet*) 13
14. The road to Donegal 14
15. Full circle (*duet*) 15
16. Thirsty work 16
17. Farewell to Skye 17
18. Lady Katherine's pavane 17
19. Dance of the Sugar Plum Fairy (Tchaikovsky) 18
20. Allegro in A (Telemann) 18
21. Still reeling 19
22. Mexican fiesta 20
23. Show stopper 20
24. Spy movie 21
25. Largo, from the *New World* Symphony (Dvořák) (*duet*) 22
26. Hornpipe, from the *Water Music* (Handel) 23
27. Hungarian folk dance 24
28. Wild West 25
29. Midnight song 26
30. Wade in the water 27
31. Dominant gene (*duet*) 28
32. Chromatic cats 29
33. Show off! 29
34. Little lamb 30
35. Habanera, from *Carmen* (Bizet) 31
36. Alleluia (Boyce) 32
37. Jubilate Deo (Mozart) 32
38. Round Trinidad Bay 32

1 2
1. Ready to rock
KB & DB
Determined
f
5
9
ff
13
mp
cresc.
ff

3 4
2. Clear skies
KB & DB
Relaxed
2
mp
7
11
cresc.
15
mp
rit.
p

Also try this in 3rd position using the fingering given.

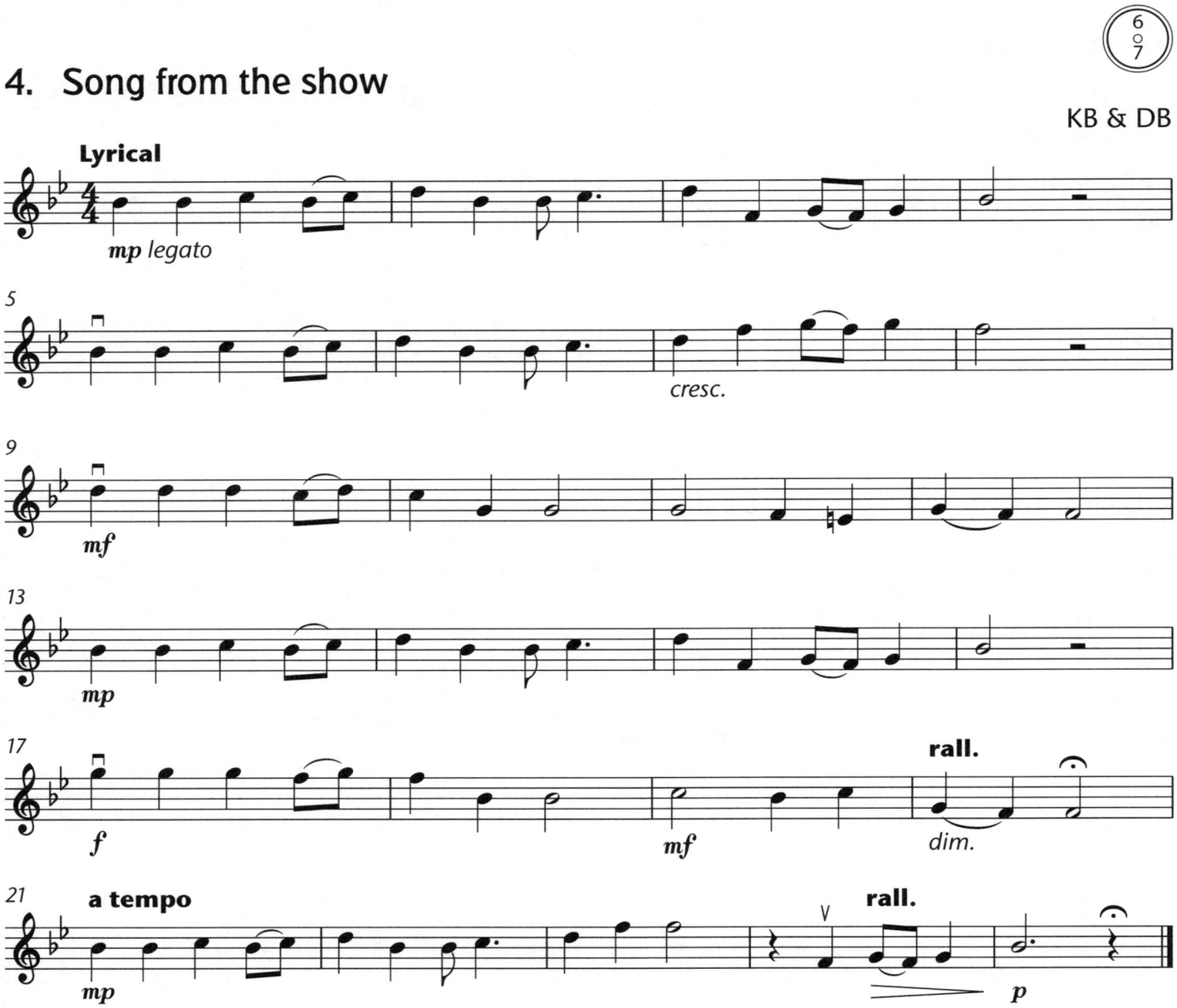
6
7
4. Song from the show
KB & DB
Lyrical
mp legato
5
cresc.
9
mf
13
mp
17
f
mf
rall.
dim.
21
a tempo
mp
rall.
p

8
9
5. Starry night
KB & DB
Tenderly
mp espress.
6
11

6. Paris café

10 ○ 11

KB & DB

7. Gaudete!

Medieval carol

8. Jacob's dance

9. Sprint finish

L 17 ○ 18 R

10. Bolero

Spanish trad.

This piece can be played as a solo or duet with piano, or as an unaccompanied violin duet.

11. William Tell

G. A. Rossini (1792–1868)

Warm up

Repeat an octave higher.

12. Country gardens

English Morris Dance tune

13. You and me

L 22 R
KB & DB
Happy
f
f
4
5
4
9
ff
mp cresc.
ff
mp cresc.
13
f
ff
You and me!
f
ff

14. The road to Donegal

KB & DB

Warm up

Try a G major scale/arpeggio with hooked bowing.

L 25 R
15. Full circle
KB & DB
Gently
mp
mp
9
mf
mf
15
mp
mp
20
25
mf
mf
29
cresc.
cresc.
rit.
f
f

16. Thirsty work

KB & DB

Chorus

Lively

mf sempre staccato

5 Verse 1

mf

9 Chorus

mf

13 Verse 2

mp

cresc.

17 Chorus

mf

Variation: the chorus and verse 1 can be played in semiquavers with spiccato bowing.

Warm ups

sim.

spiccato

Repeat on the A and E strings.

17. Farewell to Skye

28 ○ 29

KB & DB

18. Lady Katherine's pavane

30 ○ 31

KB & DB

The pavane was a slow, stately court dance popular in the 16th and 17th centuries.

19. Dance of the Sugar Plum Fairy

(from the *Nutcracker* ballet)

P. I. Tchaikovsky (1840–93)

Andante

p sempre stacc.

mf

p

f

20. Allegro in A

G. P. Telemann (1681–1767)

Allegro

f (p)

mp

cresc.

mf

f

Try starting this piece with either a down or an up bow.

21. Still reeling

(based on *Blair Atholl*, trad. Scottish reel)

Add your own dynamics to this reel.

A second player could add a drone accompaniment using these two chords; how about a drum/bodhran rhythm too?

38 ○ 39

22. Mexican fiesta

KB & DB

Use these words to help with the rhythm:

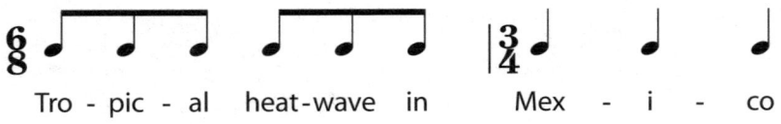

40 ○ 41

23. Show stopper

KB & DB

42 ○ 43

24. Spy movie

KB & DB

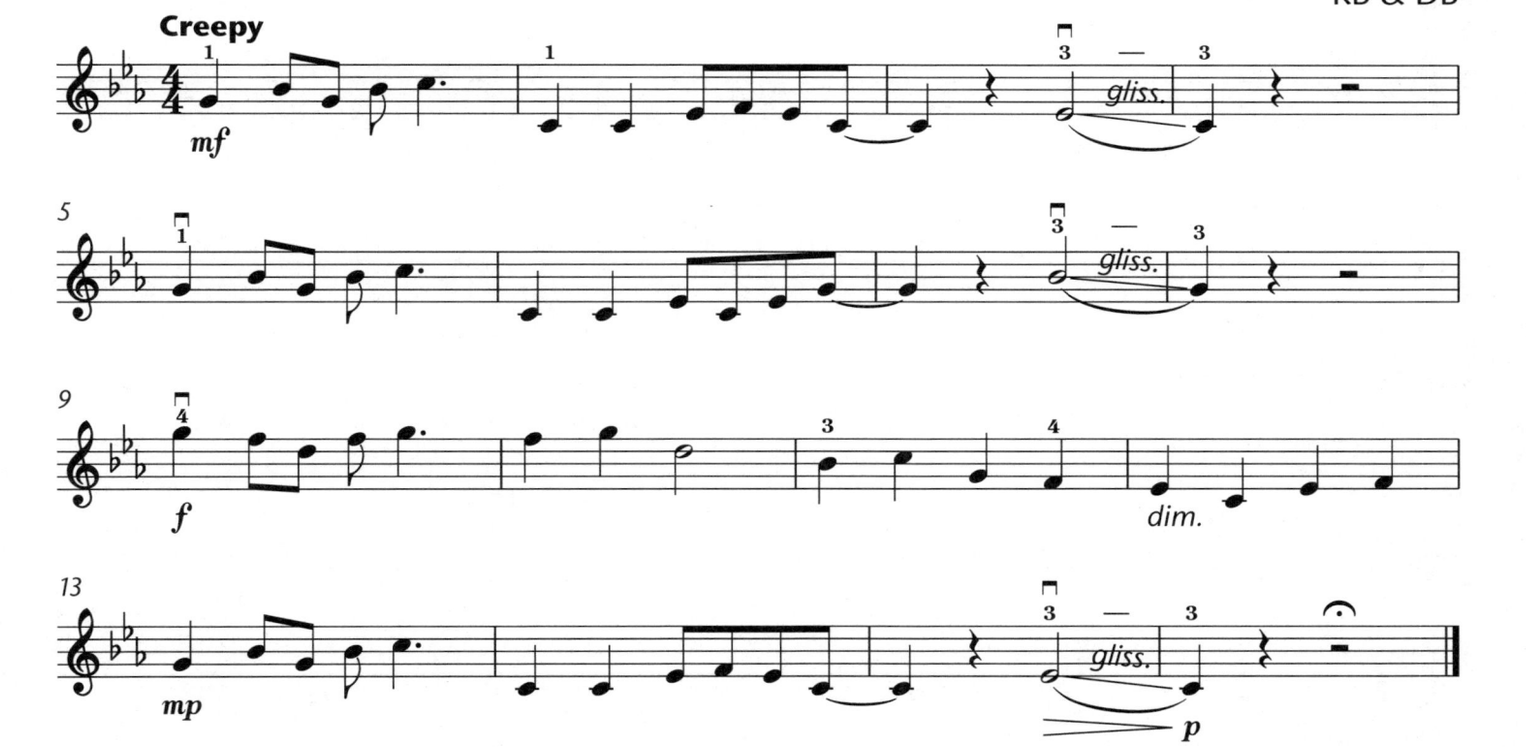

25. Largo

(from the *New World* Symphony)

Antonin Dvořák (1841–1904)

26. Hornpipe

(from the *Water Music*)

G. F. Handel (1685–1759)

27. Hungarian folk dance

KB & DB

Warm ups

Try these two warm ups in the Lydian mode.

28. Wild West

KB & DB

Warm up

Use this warm up to practise changing quickly from 1st to 3rd position.

29. Midnight song

KB & DB

Warm up

Practise legato shifts from 1st to 3rd position with this warm up.

Also try on the D and E strings.

30. Wade in the water

Spiritual

Insistent

(piano bass)

3

mp

8

12

4

4

mf

16

4

4

f

20

(1

2)

1

mf

mf

25

0

29

2

mp

4

Slower

4

rall.

1

2

p espress.

Warm ups

Sing and play this warm up a few times to get the feel of the syncopated rhythm.

Can you play a whole blues scale on D using this rhythm? (See *Fiddle Time Scales 2.*)

etc.

31. Dominant gene

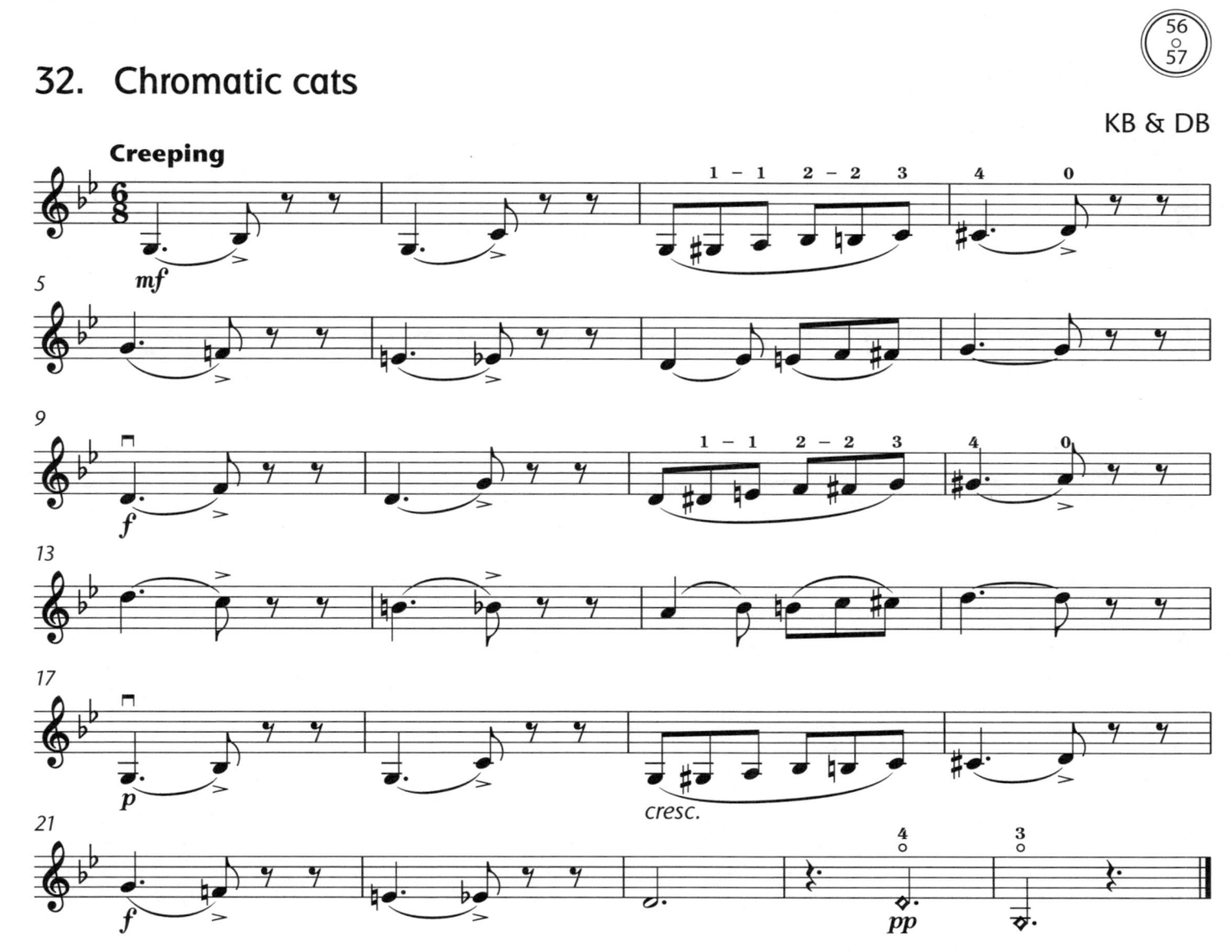
56
57
32. Chromatic cats
KB & DB
Creeping
mf
f
p
cresc.
f
pp

58
59
33. Show off!
KB & DB
Funky
f (stay in 2nd position)
ff
f
p
f

34. Little lamb

Spiritual

Warm ups

Play a C major scale in 2nd position like this:

35. Habanera

(from *Carmen*)

Georges Bizet (1838–75)

Allegretto quasi Andantino

Warm up

To get the feel of the triplet rhythm, try playing a chromatic scale on D with this pattern:

etc.

Round up

Play these rounds or canons in 2 or more parts, entering at *.

36. Alleluia

William Boyce (1711–79)

Joyfully

f

37. Jubilate Deo

W. A. Mozart (1756–91)

Allegro

f

38. Round Trinidad Bay

KB & DB

Calypso

f